Alive to Tell

*An Amputee's Story of Miraculous Survival
and the Blessings That Followed*

Denise Glenn

WestBow Press
A DIVISION OF THOMAS NELSON
& ZONDERVAN

Copyright © 2017 Denise Glenn.

All rights reserved. No part of this book may be used or reproduced by any means, graphic, electronic, or mechanical, including photocopying, recording, taping or by any information storage retrieval system without the written permission of the author except in the case of brief quotations embodied in critical articles and reviews.

THE HOLY BIBLE, NEW INTERNATIONAL VERSION®, NIV® Copyright © 1973, 1978, 1984, 2011 by Biblica, Inc.® Used by permission. All rights reserved worldwide.

WestBow Press books may be ordered through booksellers or by contacting:

WestBow Press
A Division of Thomas Nelson & Zondervan
1663 Liberty Drive
Bloomington, IN 47403
www.westbowpress.com
1 (866) 928-1240

Because of the dynamic nature of the Internet, any web addresses or links contained in this book may have changed since publication and may no longer be valid. The views expressed in this work are solely those of the author and do not necessarily reflect the views of the publisher, and the publisher hereby disclaims any responsibility for them.

Any people depicted in stock imagery provided by Thinkstock are models, and such images are being used for illustrative purposes only. Certain stock imagery © Thinkstock.

ISBN: 978-1-5127-7338-5 (sc)
ISBN: 978-1-5127-7339-2 (hc)
ISBN: 978-1-5127-7337-8 (e)

Library of Congress Control Number: 2017901308

Print information available on the last page.

WestBow Press rev. date: 2/17/2017

Preface

Everyone, at some time or another, will experience some type of mishap, setback or tragic incident that will leave them hurt, angry or drastically changed forever. We are humans and that goes along with this world we live in. It's just a fact. Although the events in my story were catastrophic, I want you to know that the Lord doesn't view our problems as big or small. He cares what we are going through and doesn't weigh them on our human scale of complaint worthy or not. He is always by your side, ready to help.

At the end of some speaking engagements, I often heard this statement, "My problems don't seem as big after hearing what you've been through", and perhaps my story helped them in some way. But I want to be clear. By writing or telling my story, I never intend to minimize anyone else's heartaches, brokenness, or unfortunate situations that have taken place in their lives. When it is YOU in the middle of a situation, it is a *major* event to you, and to God, no matter how trivial it may seem to someone else.

The truest statement I know is this one: "If you haven't been through it, you can't understand it". Certainly, you can sympathize, but you cannot truly empathize. This is not to say that family and friends do not play a big role in recuperation or helping with positive encouragement; but your ***attitude*** plays a much more significant role in recovery than you can comprehend. You shouldn't have to cope when you can overcome. Even though this was the most traumatic incident in my life, my dependency on God has been ongoing throughout my life. Unfortunately, we are never going to conquer one struggle and begin a perfect life. There will be constant ups and downs.

Without consulting God I married at a young age, had a baby girl (best thing about the marriage) and then divorced within three years and became a single mom, which was no easy task. I praise all of you who are in that stage. Keep looking up. God knows your struggles and He will provide the finances, food and the right man. Then, after consulting God about the matter (which you should always do first), I married a wonderful, Christian man, Pete. When things began to fall into place, I miscarried our first child. The emotional and physical scars were there. The pain seemed unbearable at times.

The only thing that pulled me through those events, and all others since, has been Jesus. Beyond all the bad things that were all around at that time in my life, the outcome is what kept my focus. I knew I would get through it with God's help, and I did. And it was not merely getting by, but overcoming in a big way.

Let me use a play on words right now. It may seem silly to you but will bring a smile to your face and give a whole new meaning to the word forever after when you hear it. God likes big BUTS! Now, read the word again; buts, with one 't'. Yes, I'm smiling, and you are probably chuckling. He does. All through scripture you read how a certain situation could have occurred, BUT God had a different idea. The enemy could have won the battle, BUT God was in charge and had another plan. He loves to prove himself faithful and loving and can change any situation for the better. (Genesis 50:20, a favorite verse and testimony of faith that I will share later).

As you read this you will see the times of humor, yes humor, amidst the bleak reality of it all, and see the miracle of timing by God in many moments. I, personally, do not believe in luck, karma or coincidence. If something good comes to you it is a blessing from God. If it is something difficult, it is a situation *allowed* by the Lord for a purpose and a teaching moment. We may not understand why, but one day we will.

If you've asked Jesus into your heart and are a child of God, you know this truth. If you don't know Jesus in a personal way, meet me at the end of this book to see just how easy that is to do. I believe there is a reason this book is in your hands right now and with one simple prayer you can make a fresh start to your new journey.

So, I will pray you will find hope and encouragement as you read this, and know… **you are never alone**.

Introduction

In January, 1990, someone in our church asked for prayer for a young, 16-year-old girl who had lost her leg in an accident. She was working at a carwash in town, which entailed jumping into the cars as they finished and driving them out to be hand detailed. She had accidentally slipped while getting into the car and the chain pulling the car grabbed her leg and had severed her foot and part of her leg.

My heart ached for this young girl and I could not get her out of my mind. I felt God telling me to go and pray with her. I did pray for her (in the comfort of my home), but dismissed going to see her. After all, I knew nothing about amputations and didn't know how I could possibly cheer her up, so I continued my regular routines. During the next few weeks, however, everywhere I went I was constantly reminded that I wasn't doing God's will. I watched TBN and they were talking about obedience and listening to God's promptings. The preacher talked about procrastination and not putting off until later what can be done now. The radio station would play excerpts from missionaries about not making excuses to

God and play songs about telling people about Jesus and how he loved them.

After realizing this bombardment had a purpose, and that God was trying to wrap me on the head and get my attention (guess I'm not a fast learner), I listened. With some trepidation, I made an appointment with her mother and took my baby girl with me as an ice breaker.

When I arrived, to my surprise, I met a sweet, teenage girl who was upbeat and positive. She told me all about her accident, and how excited she was to be getting her new 'leg'. It would have an ankle that would adjust to different heel heights so she could wear high heels; and she had to quickly learn how to walk with it because prom was coming up and she had a hot date. I just couldn't believe it. She exuded joy and confidence, not at all what I expected. I told her the people at our church had been praying for her, which she said she appreciated. She played with the baby awhile, I prayed with her and her mother and after about an hour I left. I was glad I went but still had no idea why I felt so compelled to go. Now, fast forward 6 months and you will see God's incredible timing and why I was so very glad I submitted myself to his calling.

1

This day was not unlike any other June day in Florida. Blazing hot, with a slight breeze to make it somewhat bearable. School was out for my oldest daughter Courtney, who would soon be 10, and we had big plans for the summer. I was co-leader of a girl scout troop, and our troop had just returned from a trip to Stone Mountain, Georgia, where we hiked up the mountain and had a wonderful time. I was also a leader in Missionettes and Sunday school at our church, and we were gearing up for vacation bible school. Our MOPS group (Mothers of Pre-Schoolers) was planning an outing for the younger children and this included my soon to be three-year-old, Brittany. Courtney was in gymnastics and was preparing for a meet on the following Saturday. Our calendar was very full, not unlike many who have a whole summer with their kids. (Shout out to all the moms who are multi-taskers. Oh wait, I believe that's *all* moms).

I'd been looking for little jobs to do with my girls to earn a little money for our weekend out of town (I love an opportunity to learn hard work pays off), when our scout leader called me. She injured her back and wondered if I would like to take over the job. It happened to be a part time gig helping Southern Bell deliver phone books to residents in our large metropolis. You could pick your days and choose areas close to your vicinity. I jumped at the chance. I could take the girls with me and do it at my leisure.

I chose Thursday to start and see if it would fly with the girls. It was a shorts and flip flop day with something different to do and we were excited. We drove to the pickup location where I signed a paper, not really reading the lengthy sheet, and received my book, pamphlets and map. GPS wasn't around back then and you actually had to read and decipher. It was the perfect job. There was a sheet explaining all of the extra data in the phone book, i.e., discount coupons for companies, maps for new areas, etc., and they needed to be inserted into the phone book. Yes, even a two-year-old can do that! Fortunately for me, Brittany was easily entertained when her big sister was around, so off we went on our adventure.

My grid was close by and minimal in size. I decided to give Brittany the job of handing the sheets to her sister, whereupon Courtney would place them inside the front cover and stack for me to choose from after depleting my initial bundle. It worked like a charm. We were done quickly and returned the check off list to the facility, deciding to return for a second day.

The next day was Friday, June 22, 1990. The weather repeated itself and we were able to park under the only tree shading the side of the cul-de-sac.

The girls were a little more restless today and getting thirsty. My mission was to simply finish. "Don't stop until the job is completed!" I believe I heard once or twice growing up. So, against Courtney's persistence to leave and come back later, I pushed on.

At this moment, the girls were sitting on the back of our mid-sized, station wagon swinging their feet back and forth waiting for my return. I finally finished and returned to my car. Keep in mind that this street was a small street. There were about 20 houses on the entire cul-de-sac.

As I returned, Courtney and I stood behind the car pushing the leftover books into the car, chatting that we were glad to be leaving for a drink. I faintly remember hearing a car start up and turning around briefly to see a man getting in a car a few driveways away. However, since that's not something that would normally trigger anything wrong, I didn't pay much attention. (I have a heightened sense of awareness to that sound now). I told the baby to get up into her car seat and get ready to leave. She did so right away for which I will be forever grateful, as that one moment of cooperation may have saved her life. I saw Brittany crawl into her seat and pull down the padded safety bar. That was to be the final image in my mind of my children for quite a while and the moment that would change my life forever.

2

I did have one last memory. You see, God in His infinite mercy sometimes sees fit to erase bad memories or times of extreme pain. And this was one of those times for me. I don't remember hearing any crash or any loud noise. And I don't remember any of the, of course, extreme pain. Some could say that it was because I was on so much medication afterwards that it messed up my brain. Now I know some of my friends may tell you my brain was like that before the accident! But in truth, I believe it was God's divine grace and the Holy Spirit taking control over the situation when I could not.

I only remember looking down at my legs as I sat upright inside the back of the car, and knowing something was not quite right. I remember wondering why my tennis shoe was upside down and something that looked like ribbon twirling before me.

As my mind was not able to comprehend anything at that moment, due to shock as the paramedics told me later, I still somehow knew to pray. I remember the words quite vividly and they remain the most important memory for me. And when I prayed, I did so quite loudly. I remember specifically crying out, "Lord, don't let me die. I can live without my legs, but I need to be here for my girls. Please don't let me die". After that, nothing.

The following accounts of the accident were told to me by the first responders, police and husband after I recovered.

While I was oblivious to the chaos around me, my daughter Courtney had been helping me push the phone books into the car when we were hit by a car from behind. I had been standing upright leaning in; however, because she was smaller, she was inside the back of the car with one leg up further inside and the other hanging outside.

The man I saw getting in a car, only 21 years old, was the driver. I found out later that he was living with a girlfriend at her mother's house on that street, had no car of his own, and had two suspended licenses prior to this incident. (I now have a very vocal opinion regarding people who knowingly drive with a suspended license, and the absence of working laws). He was breaking up with his girlfriend, had taken her car and was moving out with his cat. He had also been smoking marijuana, as a still lit remnant was in the car when the ambulance arrived.

I have never owned a cat; however, several cat owners tell me that cats are not particularly fond of car travel and sometimes become erratic. This was the case that day. Apparently, the young man departed his driveway just two driveways away from our car and drove down the street at what the police calculated was around 30 miles an hour. From the young man's account, his cat became scared. He had one hand on the wheel and when he turned around with the other hand to calm or grab the cat, he veered into the back of my car. It hit with such impact that it crushed my legs and then bounced backward, slamming me and Courtney into the inside of our car (which we believe may have caused her diagnosis of scoliosis in 8th grade).

My mid-size station wagon was buckled like a V and the impact blew out the windows on the sides shattering glass everywhere. Courtney's right leg which had been outside the car was badly injured. The impact broke her leg in multiple places and almost took her heel completely off. Still, she had enough clear-headedness in the situation to hold it onto her foot until help arrived. Of course, this was while she saw me with all the trauma to my legs; and as she told me later, yelling that my legs were on fire. Because Brittany was in her seat and held in place, the shattered glass was in her hair and on her clothes but physically she was unharmed; the emotional toll was a different thing.

As any mother will tell you, you never want your children to go through anything upsetting or traumatic; but if they do, you want to reassure them that you will be there for them and everything will be okay. In this instance, I could do neither.

My girls knew no one there and were placed in a situation of strangers all around, which was a dangerous predicament all its own. I was unaware of anything. It was something that broke my heart and brought me to tears when I was helpless for several months to do anything for my precious girls.

To convey the severity of the scene and physical issues without being too graphic is hard to do. I could be more detailed, but just picture the worst-case scenario in order to understand all of the incredible things that happened next throughout my and my daughter's recovery. It was obviously traumatic, but also seemed like a hopeless and devastating situation to everyone involved.

Yes, a really awful thing happened. **BUT**, (remember that word?), God was there with us in the midst of it all. I read a post that is so true and relevant for everyone. In effect, it says that at some point in time we will all face situations that seem to overwhelm us and defeat us. We may even ask God why it is happening to us. But remember, when life seems out of control and you are in the middle of an evil attack of any kind, realize that the matter is not over yet. If you keep your eyes on the Lord, He will turn the situation around to your good. Impossible? Well, you'll have to wait for it, but I promise the good is coming. Just keep reading my friend.

*J. Todd Hostetler, cityonahill.org- July 20, 2013

3

Many things occurred in a short amount of time around the accident scene. The man was so panicked he left his car running and ran to the nearest door knocking frantically. When the woman opened the door, he yelled, "Call 911!" and fled the scene. As inhumane as his actions sound, that became the **first blessing** of the day because he took the time to notify someone. This allowed the woman to call sooner so help could respond quicker.

Second blessing - remember there are no coincidences as far as I'm concerned. The woman who came to the door was the first on the scene and she happened to be a retired critical care nurse. God is so good! You just can't make this stuff up!

She called 911 and assessed the scene to tell them the problems. She talked to me and Courtney and was able to make Courtney feel better until the ambulance arrived. Her other neighbor, **third blessing**, was the young mother of a baby the same age as Brittany. She took Brittany off to the side, away from the accident, so she would be distracted by playing with her daughter.

As the first responders arrived, the **fourth blessing** occurred. Courtney, being shoved into this mess with strangers all around, was understandably scared and nervous. But as the ambulance drivers exited their vehicles, she recognized one of the men walking around the corner. Out of all of the EMT's in our huge city, God chose to send the husband of her gymnastics coach who worked part time as a first responder. Today was one of his days. Mr. D.J., as the kids called him, hugged her and was able to reassure her and get her and her sister into a separate ambulance. Jeff Lott and the men of "C" shift did an incredible job that day helping save my life.

I have to tell you, when that was told to me, my heart was so full of thankfulness to my Savior. He knew I couldn't be there for them at that time so he came in the way of D.J. and other compassionate men. If you know a firefighter or EMT, please shake their hand and tell them how much you appreciate the tireless, sometimes underappreciated work they do. They don't do it because they have to, they choose to because they want to make a difference.

I hope, somehow, they read this someday and realize how grateful I am. I could never express my thanks enough for helping me and my girls that day.

So far, God had orchestrated all the people I needed for that exact moment in time. Do you still believe in coincidence? And that wasn't all of the miracles. It's been many years now and I am still smiling when I think about those miracles of love sent to little 'ol me, by a mighty God who loves me unconditionally. He is more than able to do GREAT things. And He will do them for you too!

4

No one wants to get that awful call from a hospital or police department departing devastating news, but they happen. Such was the case when the police called my husband, Pete. We had only been married 5 years, were planning to have another baby soon and we were looking forward to many happy, fulfilled years.

When the policeman called him from the scene and told him I was in an accident, he said he heard what sounded like me yelling. He found out later, as you will in the story, what the 'yelling' was about and how that played a part in that moment.

As they contacted Pete, he was told we were being taken to University Hospital (now U. F. Health Jacksonville) which was and still remains a major trauma hospital in our area, but was not told the extent of any of our injuries. As the initial news was given, he heard 'University' and headed toward another hospital on University Boulevard. This would have been the right assumption since it was very close to the accident scene. But when he arrived, they said they had no one by our names that had come in and upon checking other area hospitals, he was directed to the correct one.

He had no idea how badly we were injured, but when he heard the correct hospital name he realized it was the trauma hospital and it must be serious. Once at the correct hospital, he explained to the front desk nurse that his wife and two daughters were brought by ambulance and asked to see them. As he tells it, no one would tell him anything other than my older daughter and myself were being evaluated. (He later found out that actually meant being prepped for surgery). When he became a little more vocal, he was taken to the pediatric unit where he saw Brittany on a bed being talked to by two nurses. She looked and acted fine, and when he tried to ask Brittany what happened, she told him, "Mommy got runned over by a car". He then realized something of major significance had happened.

As he came around the corner with Brittany to wait for answers, the **fifth blessing** came walking in. It was our friend from church who worked in that unit. Brittany knew her and she quickly led them into her office. I'm not sure how she found out but she actually went looking for Pete. She even watched Brittany so Pete could find out about Courtney's condition and mine. When he saw Courtney, she had been sedated and was heading to surgery but knew he was there. Her leg was broken in multiple places and her heel was barely hanging on. Most of her fascia (padding) was gone and her Achilles tendon would have to be repaired.

The next information from the surgeon was simply terrifying. He was told that I was critical, may have internal bleeding and that I was going to lose *both* legs. **Both**. One was too badly crushed and the other too badly broken. I ask you… How do you handle that kind of news within an hour of sitting at your desk having a normal day? And they asked if I could possibly be pregnant? We were trying for another baby, so now there was fear of possibly losing an unborn child. (I was not pregnant, which was a good thing in this bad situation). The most inconsequential of my injuries was the missing half of my front tooth which wasn't considered a priority in the chaos.

When he came to see me, I was pumped with morphine and didn't realize he was there. He could see the sheet over my legs and that they were in plastic ice bags. But he remembers knowing that the one area under the sheet looked as if nothing was there. He knew it was bad. As he went out to wait, his initial thoughts were, if she loses both legs, what will she do? How will she function? And of course, these are normal thoughts when you have never been through or know anyone who has been through this situation.

Still numb and having signed papers to begin Courtney's surgery, he called the church and then had to make another important call that I know he dreaded making. My parents were living in south Florida at the time, and he called them trying not to sound too despondent. He told them I was in intensive care from an accident. I am the first, middle and last child of my parents. Yes, an only child. So maybe I was a little spoiled, I can't say. But I was always loved and cherished by my doting parents, and even as an adult that didn't change. They were packed and on their way within the hour.

In an instant, his whole world had changed. I can't imagine, other than shedding tears, the emotions that ran through his head. All I know is that he never gave up on me or us as a family unit, despite all of the things we were about to experience. He overcame with me; and after 32 years of marriage, he's still a keeper.

5

As they readied me for surgery and were examining me for other potential issues, the on call orthopedic surgeon gave a call to the head of Orthopedics to consult. That doctor's name was Dr. Horowitz. **6th blessing** had arrived. This was Dr. Horowitz's day off, but as he was checking on the status of another patient, he was called to the trauma unit to give his expert advice on a patient who was brought in with severe leg injuries and possibly internal bleeding. Me. He was one of the first doctors to use the external fixator. This was an instrument that sets pins internally and attaches to an outside metal structure when there are too many bones broken to cast. Also, the skin had been completely removed on my shin leaving the bone exposed. (Which later would call for a separate surgery to skin graft.)

The on-call doctor said he believed both legs were too badly damaged to save. **BUT** ☺ … Dr. Horowitz said "no". The one leg was almost completely severed, but he believed he could save my other leg. So… **on his day off**… he scrubbed up and went into surgery with his entourage to save my leg.

Dr. Horowitz gave credence to the possibility of saving one young mother's leg, and he ended up accomplishing just that. When others thought it was impossible, God used him as an instrument to prove it could be done. In Mark 10:27, Jesus says, "With people it is impossible, but not with God; for all things are possible with God." He is soooo worthy of our praise!

Whatever it was that made him choose to stay and help, I'll never know; but with that one compassionate and kind decision, things changed for the better. Although he is now deceased, he was an angel of mercy that day and I believe the Lord planned the steps for that extraordinarily, talented doctor to be in the hospital at that exact moment when I needed him the most.

The surgery took many hours, of course, and Pete said that our pastors and friends from church practically took over the waiting room. Praying, talking and simply being there for us. They wouldn't even have had to speak a word; their presence said it all. My girl scout troop and MOPS group ladies came as well. Everyone was praying for our family. Pete hadn't called them yet, only family, as he was still processing it all, and talking with the doctors as they made their decisions. So how did they know?

Remember him hearing me yell at the accident? **Blessing number 7.** According to one of the EMT's, although in shock and not really coherent, not only did I pray but I was rattling off phone numbers and names of people to call for prayer. That is truly a miracle because as I am today, totally coherent, I can't remember relevant numbers without checking my phone. That is where God assisted again and helped me relay the information. You couldn't make a quick cell phone call back then, but between our nurse friend calling and my yelling, the calls went out slowly but made their way out none the less.

Pete was overwhelmed with the response of the number of people who came. Some of the women from our church had been on a women's retreat and had just returned to hear the news. By early evening my parents had arrived to find out the details and that they had already taken my right leg just below my knee. My mother, understandably, was a basket case as was my dad, steadfast as he was trying to be. As natural as a mother's love is for her kids, there is something to say about dads. I was my daddy's girl and for him not to be able to fix this was a heartbreak in itself.

I had a tib/fib fracture (tibia, fibula bones) of my left leg. Since the bone was broken in multiple places and had severe skin and muscle loss, it couldn't be cast as a normal break. The external fixator was put in place with four pins. Three in my shin; one just below my knee, the other in the middle section and the third near my ankle. The final one was in my foot. There was also a plate with screws placed above my ankle for extra support for the bone.

Then a muscle flap procedure was performed. That is a technique where they dissect your muscle and pull a partial piece around to add a layer of muscle where there is none. This is to provide bulk that can fill a deeper defect, which in this case was over my shin bone where the skin was taken off by the force of the impact. This led to the third surgery - the skin graft surgery to cover the shin bone on my 'good leg'.

The saving of this leg came with many complications and throughout it all, I became accustomed to many terms associated with orthopedic problems and amputations.

My amputated leg was aptly called my 'residual limb' because it was what remained of my God given leg. And because it was below the knee, the terminology was a 'BK amputation' for short. With this amputation, I experienced what is known as 'phantom pain'. This is when you have no limb left but the nerves tell your brain that the limb is still attached. Your brain is a powerful tool and knows how things are supposed to be. It is painful and can be a burning sensation or throbbing pain for others. In my case, it was the latter. For example, I could actually feel and pinpoint the exact toe that was hurting even though my toe was no longer there. Sometimes cold or warm compresses helped, but there was no medical explanation other than nerves going crazy and no remedy. Sounds weird, but something you deal with all of your life in some cases. And it can be especially hard on the elderly.

I found out later that although I lost my leg, had it been an amputation alone and no trauma to my other leg, I would only have been in the hospital for three to five days. As it turned out, there were many complications with my 'saved' leg and I was to remain in the hospital for several months.

When it came time for the surgery to my other leg, I was told by the plastic surgeon what the skin graft would entail. The procedure involved taking a thin piece of skin from another fatty part of your body, in my case my thigh, and adding it to the muscle to graft onto and grow. Also, he said if my broken bones didn't fuse or heal properly due to being older… Older? I was 32 and didn't consider myself old… then a *bone* graft may have to be done within the next year.

Now, mind you, I had incredible doctors and always a team of interns around as this was a teaching hospital. However, doctors give you the facts as *they* see them and as a Christian, I go by 2 Corinthians 5:7, "We walk by faith and not by sight". I am a believer in speaking out loud those things that you hope for and have faith to believe the Lord will take care of you. Also, Psalm 121:1,2 were pertinent to me at my time of trial and pain and verses I hold dear still. "I will lift my eyes unto the hills where my help comes from. My help comes from the Lord, who made the heavens and the earth".

So, I boldly told the doctor that no bone graft would be necessary and that my leg would heal just fine. He smiled and said he hoped so, but felt it important for me to know for the future.

I found out a few days later when a hospital psychologist came to see me, that the doctor sent her because he said I was 'in denial' about the condition of my leg. Bless his heart. If he would have only realized that I know the Great Physician and nothing is impossible with God!

6

As I was in the hospital for several months. I did get quite homesick and frustrated with things and missed my girls. It was especially hard not seeing Courtney and only hearing how she was doing from Pete. I wanted to see her and hug her. I wanted to explain what was going on with me and that we would be fine. Because Courtney and I couldn't be moved from our beds, the kind nurses brought Courtney up in her bed to see me and put our beds side by side so we could visit. It was the highlight of my stay. Courtney was upset when she saw my legs, but saw me in good spirits and felt the hugs. Her mama was still here to do that. She also came to realize God would get us through this. But this visit only happened because of the many compassionate people who worked there, which God specifically placed around me to help.

I was on the 8th floor trauma unit and because of the length of my stay, I got to know many of the employees there; two in particular. The D.O.N. (Director of Nursing) for the unit was a Christian woman. Another blessing in my eyes. She was 'on her game' with her nurses and always knew what was going on. She would always check on me herself before she ended her shift; and I remember a special day when she came in on a Sunday all dressed up from church and gave me some donuts that her Sunday School class had offered. We read verses together and prayed for God's healing touch. This was not her day to work but she came to see me. The impact of her kindness will forever remain with me.

I also met and befriended one of the sweet, morning custodians. He would talk to me and constantly uplift me with each subsequent surgery. I always kidded with him as I was leaving for more procedures and tell him he couldn't get rid of me that easily; that I was merely hanging around to chat with him more. Then he would add that he was looking forward to my final departure to be with my family.

Although through the years my mind can't remember their names, I vividly remember their kind faces and all the things they didn't have to do, but blessed me immeasurably by doing them anyway. I don't know if they were given much recognition by other patients, but they always came with a smile. That's something we can all do. A smile costs nothing, but the impact can be priceless! When words cannot be spoken, a smile can break through any barrier.

The help we received was above and beyond anything imaginable. My parents stayed for a week and when my father went back to work, my aunt came down and stayed with my mom to help with the girls. Our friends became our support team, helping more than we could have imagined. The women from our church were beyond incredible, as were the MOPS women and girl scouts' moms. They cooked meals for Pete and the girls while I was hospitalized, lasting the entire three months. They took the girls to events and even did some laundry. You know you have special friends when they can discern what things need to be done without being asked. My father once told me, "You can count yourself lucky if you can count your good friends on more than one hand". And our friends came through in a big way. Our neighbors actually brought a turkey and all the fixings for Thanksgiving that year. Those kinds of friends are rare and I try wholeheartedly to be one. Always try to see the need before it is spoken, because most of the time no one wants to ask for help.

I personally think God knows everyone needs help at some point and he places people around you so that you can receive a blessing. Don't rob someone of their blessing by being stubborn. Take the help. You can always return the favor later. And it's a lot of fun to think of ways to do it!

7

Now my husband Pete is the constant kidder, sometimes joking with dry humor that only I recognize. However, people that know him understand and appreciate his lighter side. And I, or so I have been told, have a pretty good attitude when looking at trials. There is no point in being angry or despondent about things you cannot change, even though I surely had some moments, and I try to look at the brighter side; the big scheme of things.

I was on Morphine for about three weeks until I fully knew what was going on and many people came to visit me during that time. Although I could talk to people and carry on a conversation, I didn't remember the previous day's events or even the visits afterwards because of the medications. I was in a room by a window which, being a lover of nature, was wonderful for me; and I remember the one thing that made me relaxed from pain or thinking about being there was having my hair brushed. As a woman, trying to look good in a hospital is almost impossible, especially when you have hair that needs washing. Right?

Anyway, some friends came one Sunday afternoon to visit and I talked to them and chatted while Pete acted as my salon stylist. They commented on how he was doting on me and giving me such attention, when his response came that made everyone laugh. He answered saying, "I'm glad to do it. She says it makes her feel relaxed. And she's on morphine, so if I accidentally pull too hard she won't feel any pain. And she may not remember the nice things you are saying about me tomorrow, so you may want to come back again. It can be like a brand-new visit!" Yes, that's my Pete. He goes right along with the flow.

Not to say he didn't have his share of hard times with all of this. He was coming on lunch break every day to visit Courtney and me. He also had to be trained to do a sterile dressing change for debridement of the skin on the wound. You can look it up if you are inclined, but I won't go into what all that entails. Needless to say, it is very painful to the patient but necessary for the skin to heal properly. Even though it was painful, I was grateful that he could do it and not the nurses, because I knew he was being as careful as he could not to hurt me. It is part of the nurses' duty and although they were kind, they had to do what needed to be done knowing pain would come with it. He was also coming back a night, showering, staying overnight and then heading straight back to work in the mornings. He did this almost the entire time which became another hardship which I will explain in a bit.

He also had to make special arrangements for Courtney's school work and later special arrangements with the school for after school care until he could pick her up. Meanwhile, he was trying to find someone to watch Brittany after my mom and dad returned home. He was a busy guy, but I never remember him complaining. Sometimes people look at the patient and don't give any regard to the impact these significant changes have on the family. Always remember, there may be one victim or patient, but that person has a family who has felt the effects as well.

I want to also mention that I have had encounters with other amputees that have had to deal with extra burdens after their initial trauma. Some of them had a loved one divorce them afterwards, or worse, simply leave because they couldn't handle the changes that were happening to *their* life, not the amputee's life. Yes, it does happen, but don't be too critical of them. It takes a mighty strong person to handle all the burdens and changes from something like that all at once. You never know how you would handle a situation if you were the family member or the patient. And it is so much harder if you don't have the Lord to lean on and someone who you know will be with you through the hard times. I trusted that the love Pete and I had was strong enough to get us through that, and it was.

8

As the days rolled on and I was past the surgeries, I was nearing the end of my stay. It all depended on the healing process of my 'good' leg and, at the moment, it was doing well. I had started therapy which was not the highlight of my day. The hydro therapy was to help with the debridement process as well. It was every day and hurt quite a bit. The therapy room was not large and was segmented by several curtains and a couple of separate rooms. On one side were large pools for an entire body, for burn victims I was told. The others were smaller basins for other extremities such as mine. I could put my leg in it from my wheelchair.

There were many people in the therapy room each time I came and I made it a point to keep my gaze downward. I knew how I felt, and I did look pretty pitiful. My one leg was missing, while the other had a huge metal monstrosity projecting from it. No one wants to be viewed as different; and while I was not in a good way, I saw so many more who were worse off than me. Being in a large city there are always victims of some crisis, but I was never as close to the physical suffering of others as I was when in therapy.

I vividly remember one woman who came into the hospital from a fire. I never saw her, but could hear her screams as they lowered her into the water. I cried for her. After several days of praying for her, I asked the therapist if there weren't another type of therapy that wouldn't hurt her so. She explained that when someone is burned, the layer of skin that protects the nerves is gone. Then everything that touches you is painful because you have no external barrier to the outside. Even the air would hurt her. In all my pain, I couldn't imagine hers.

Suffice to say, there are always those who are worse off than you. Pray for them and be aware of others' needs instead of focusing on your own. Not only will it take the focus off of your pain for a while, but will help you to see through the eyes of others and allow you to be of help to them in some way.

Things seemed to be progressing well and I was now at the end of my second month in the hospital. As I was eating my lunch, I felt a wetness on my leg under the covers. As I pulled the covers back, I noticed that my left leg that was wrapped between the fixator, was suddenly, and without warning, bleeding uncontrollably. The entire site of my skin graft was red. I was horrified and pushed my call button to get a nurse. I had a routine in the hospital and wasn't usually shocked by anything, but when the nurse arrived I was hysterical.

Through the tears, I showed her the bandages and asked why this may be happening. I could barely get the words out while she seemed as if she was clearly not alarmed. This was a new nurse and it felt as if she didn't care and I wanted her to get the doctor right away. She patted my hand to calm me and explained. She told me what I didn't realize was that the bleeding meant that the tissue was healthy and was healing as it should. And the next words she used meant more to me in another way. She said, "The blood means it's healing". I was immediately reminded about the healing blood of Jesus. He was my healing power. This was a moment from the Lord to show me he was still on the job! Why that time was chosen for the bleeding to begin, I don't know; but I know the result was incredible and deemed **blessing number 8**.

My mind was calmed and my soul felt at peace. Would I have chosen any of this? No. But I was not going through it alone. And I couldn't wait to share with Pete and my visitors what great things God was doing.

9

When everything seems to be going right in your life, Satan, the enemy of your soul, will bring something to upset your world. As I don't believe in coincidence or good luck, I also don't believe that bad things occur just by happenstance. The evil in this world begins with a plan that the devil hatches to ruin our chances and purpose in this world. God's word, the bible, says that his only purpose is to steal, kill and destroy, and it brings the devil much pleasure. **BUT** Jesus came so that you could have life and live it to the fullest! I don't believe anyone would choose the first over the latter; but on this day, it seemed evil was coming in a big way.

I was feeling good knowing I would be going home soon. My nurse finished taking her routine set of vitals and I was watching reruns of my favorite show - M.A.S.H. (I watched it as much as I could and it gave me the medicine I needed… Laughter). I heard a knock on the door and presumed a friend had come to visit. In walked a young woman with a hospital badge, but not a nurse. I then thought she was coming with paperwork for my upcoming departure.

She introduced herself as a representative from the financial department of the hospital. She handed me a form and said it was something that didn't need attention at the moment but that I should discuss it with my husband when he arrived. She explained that even though we had insurance, the amount of hospital fees and all other related fees would be a large amount and that usually people don't have that amount of money to be able to pay. It turned out to be a form from the hospital stating that because of the enormous amount of money I would owe, a lien was being put on our house! In short, we would have to sign the agreement using our house as collateral if we were delinquent on the bill or unable to pay the hospital off. Once again, I went from high on the mountaintop to down in the valley. The woman was very professional and to the point and then left the paperwork with me to consult with my husband.

This is not what you want to see when you are trying to think positively about getting better. I admit the feelings I had at that moment were many. Anger toward the woman for telling me this while I was alone, worry for Pete who was already working so hard on one small income to provide (although very grateful he had a job), and yes, feeling as if God had forgotten me.

Looking back, I can't believe I thought that after all of the miracles He had provided so far. Just being alive should have been the clincher. But, I am only human. We all are. And when it seems as if the hardships are non-stop, in our human frailness we don't see the bigger picture. Remember, God knew all along what I would go through and the outcome. He is never surprised.

So, as I sat crying again, I tried to figure out how to tell Pete before he came for his schedule lunch visit. When he arrived, I immediately showed him the paperwork. He was furious that someone had given that paper to me without him being there but said not to worry, things would work out. At the time, I didn't see how. According to the form, my bills were almost $30,000 and mounting. (No, I was not having a faith building moment). I really had to focus on getting out of there, he said, and then we would tackle it together. He just wanted to focus on getting me home. In that moment, I saw Pete as the gem God had provided for me. That news was a hard thing to swallow in and of itself; but the timing became more significant than I realized, although he never let on.

Pete didn't tell me until after I was home, but his boss was demanding he be at work on a regular schedule. He had used all his vacation time and sick leave. When I mentioned above how so many people helped out with the girls and were of great support to us, they never knew how much of an impact they were in helping Pete be able to work as much as he was able. He was put into a position of being fired or quitting. His boss hired a man temporarily to help Pete, but was intending to hire him and replace Pete. He needed someone who could make sure the projects were continued while Pete was out and was going to replace Pete. Such turmoil should never exist in cases like this, but they do. Understandably a boss needs his employees to complete their work, but Pete was trying to work most Saturdays if he couldn't make the required time during the weekdays. He didn't want it said of him that he was ever fired from a job.

The stress must have been overwhelming; and to not be able to turn to your spouse for support and pray together must have been unbearable, but he told no one. He was already storming the gates of heaven with prayer. Now there was one more reason to turn to God. The bible says pray without ceasing (1 Thessalonians 5:16-18) and I really believe that was happening.

Thinking of the lien alone, I couldn't focus on a happy homecoming no matter what I tried. Now I became focused on possibly losing our home. Where would we go with our girls? Would I be able to get a job somehow and help with the payments? And what would the monthly payments be? **BUT,** God doesn't want us to worry. Paraphrasing here, he says that we shouldn't worry about tomorrow because tomorrow has enough troubles of its own. You won't help anything by worrying. I know this is easier said than done. We tend to focus on what we see in this world and happening right now. We don't see the bigger picture and can't possibly see what the future holds. The only thing you can do is seek God first for help. If you have a bible, please read the entire verses of Matthew 6: 25-34. It will give you a whole new perspective on worrying. Worrying comes from Satan, and we don't want to indulge him!

I did a lot of praying that day and into the coming weeks. I read my bible, listened to more praise music and turned to more positive thoughts. I would soon be with my family, see my precious little girls and be home. That put a smile on my face. I prayed so hard that the Lord would do something to help and that Pete wouldn't struggle with this on top of everything else. I told my closest friends what had happened with the lien and they began to pray too. Never underestimate the power of prayer.

My favorite quote by Alfred Lord Tennyson that was on my desk for years says this. "More things are wrought by prayer than this world dreams of". And it's the truth. God hears all prayers, and the bible says, "Where two or more are gathered in my name, I am there also". (Matthew 18:20). So, pray with all your might and keep praying until something happens.

There used to be a trendy acronym for our kids at church: PUSH. It stood for Pray Until Something Happens. God *ALWAYS* answers our prayers. He has three answers. <u>Yes</u>, and you are blessed with the thing you request. <u>Wait</u>, and he postpones the action for reasons unknown to you. Maybe he is giving you time to realize *he* is the one with the answer.

And, <u>No</u>. Your request is denied because it isn't in your best interest. You may find out later that if the request had come about, it would have been worse for you. That last one's a hard one. We tend to think God doesn't hear us because we don't get our way, right away or at all.

I didn't know what we would do about that bill and never dreamed there could be a good solution to this one. **BUT** God already had things worked out.

10

Within a few weeks of the discouraging letter, I had another visitor. As she knocked on my door and came in, I could see she wasn't hospital staff but not anyone I recognized. My initial, human thought was, *'great, someone giving me another surprise. Don't know if I want too many more of those'*. The bible says that God will not give you more than you can handle (meaning *with* His help). But even though my faith was dwindling and I was trying to handle it by myself, God was faithful to me with **blessing number 9**.

She introduced herself as a Workers' Compensation representative with United Distributors. This meant absolutely nothing to me as I had never heard of Workers' Compensation before. I was totally oblivious. As soon as she started speaking, I immediately thought it was another company needing money for something else. I started to cry and she quickly informed me that I shouldn't be upset because she brought good news. Good news? YEA! I could sure use some of that.

She explained that while I was delivering the phone books, I was technically 'working' for her company that distributed the Southern Bell phone books. (I mentioned in the beginning of my story that I signed a paper not really reading it. Now I read *every* contract, word for word, even if it seems time consuming).

When I signed that paper, it was a contract stating that if anything were to happen to me while in their employ, I would be **FULLY COMPENSATED FOR ANY ACCIDENTAL OCCURRENCE**. To be sure you get the magnitude of this, read that last statement again.

All of the bills now associated with my legs, surgeries AND ANY AND ALL prosthetic devices and medical equipment would be totally covered. Anything I would have had to pay would be paid by Workers' Compensation! I wouldn't have to worry about insurance deductibles, nothing at all! I had no idea about prosthetics at the time and how much they can cost, especially for a lifetime, yet the joy was indescribable. This was to include prosthetic appointments to update changes to my prosthetic leg, a wheelchair, walker, crutches, and all the supplies and creams for my leg; as well as any revisions to my real leg that were associated with the accident, such as removal of pins and screws later on.

Yes, once again, God loves those big BUTS! We had a lot to lose, **BUT** God chose to intervene in a big way. Things like this just don't happen by coincidence. We were common, middle class people with regular lives that had been completely turned upside down and sideways several times in a few months. To our earthly eyes, we couldn't really see how any good would come out of all that; but the light was beginning to show. And here is where the verse comes in that I mentioned earlier in the Preface.

It is from the story of Joseph and his brothers. You cannot understand the magnitude of his life and struggles without reading the whole story (Genesis 37-50), but I will try a brief synopsis. Joseph goes through a lot of trials - betrayed by his family, almost a murder victim, sold to traders, then sold again into slavery in the Pharaoh's palace. He was put in jail for a crime he didn't commit and was promised by a paroled cellmate that he would remind the Pharaoh he was still in there. The cellmate forgot which continued his time in jail. This spanned many years. He was finally released because God showed him what the Pharaoh's dreams meant, and he was the only one who could explain them to the Pharaoh. After interpreting the dreams, he was put in charge of all of Egypt, second only to the Pharaoh himself. Yes, that's a very small snippet and doesn't at all detail the major God appointment that was Joseph's; but in every aspect of his life, good or bad, one factor remained. He always sought God and remained strong, never turning from his faith and God blessed him for his faithfulness.

In the end, he had the most miraculous outcome and spoke these words (Genesis 50:20) to his brothers. "You intended to harm me, **BUT** God intended it for good to bring me to this position to save many people". God used those trials to accomplish a purpose for Joseph. His trials and many, many other accounts of people just like Joseph show us how marvelous and powerful our God is. And although our world is different now with a different way of life, **God is not.** He was and always remains the same. He will do the same for you today. We don't deserve the help, but God freely gives it because he loves you and cares about your future.

When I heard the words that the lady was saying, I began to cry in front of her. This time I was crying for a totally different reason. I felt a huge burden lifted from my shoulders and couldn't believe that this big blessing was coming to me. The poor woman was smiling as looking at me she knew what a relief it must have been. For all the heartache and questions, I just wanted to give God the glory.

I knew then that nothing could hinder God's plans for me and my family. Not to say that the next months and year wouldn't be challenging, but I knew through it all we wouldn't be alone.

11

It was now the end of September. I was in the hospital for what seemed like an eternity. Although I had begun relationships with the staff, I was more than ready to come home.

I finally got the 'all clear' and was allowed to leave. When I got outside and into the car, everything seemed bigger and better. The sun felt warmer, the birds sounded sweeter, the air smelled cleaner. You really don't realize what you have or how extraordinary little things can be until you don't have them.

The first place Pete took me was to a park along our Riverside area to just sit and enjoy the beauty. I hadn't really seen any of the outside world other than my window view overlooking buildings. I rolled down the window, closed my eyes and let the breeze overtake me. I felt like I had been released into a whole new world.

Even though I was out of the hospital, I still couldn't walk. I couldn't get my prosthesis right away and had the huge fixator on my left leg. It was very difficult just getting into the car. I had to slowly be lifted out of the wheelchair, usually by Pete, and turned at an angle so that the fixator wouldn't be hit. If anything hit the metal I could feel the vibrations through my bone. It was precarious, to say the least.

When I arrived home, it was the best medicine I could have asked for. My girls were elated to see me and I them. I wanted to hug them and never let go. They were apprehensive at first not knowing how to place themselves to not harm me further. Brittany only understood that she wanted in mommy's lap, however that needed to happen, and I was glad to be the recipient.

But I was so relieved to be home that I didn't fully comprehend how hard it would be to relearn everything. As a young mother of two, I really couldn't *do* that much. I couldn't cook, clean, wash dishes or clothes, or even dress myself without help. Mind you, there are many who their whole life need help with these things and do quite well. But I was and still am, a very independent person, who also has a German constitution. My great grandparents came over from Germany and their foundation for hard work and stubbornness followed to me. Sometimes that is not such a pleasant attribute, but it can be if used in the right way. For instance, it was my stubbornness that gave me my resolute 'never give up' attitude. And never, no never, tell me I CAN'T do something. Believe me, I will find a way to prove it otherwise. (With God's help and a smile, of course).

I wasn't even able to sleep in my own bed. We had to rearrange bedrooms and displace my girls so that a hospital bed could be brought in because of my legs. I was a mess. I tried to uphold my positive attitude and I did great for a while. But eventually Pete told me more about the job situation and I broke. I guess I initially thought we can't take any more. But he said to wait to hear the end.

The way this happened was so unbelievable, I could hardly believe it coming from my own husband. Pete overheard the name of the company where the 'new hire' was coming from when he was still at work. He decided to go to that place and apply for that position. The actual position required some experience that he did not have, however. He decided to go for the interview anyway. While he was there, when they mentioned the experience in that area was not on his resume, he came up with a possible solution. He made them an offer. He learned quickly, he said, and if they would show him what they needed and test him for two weeks, they could decide if they would keep him or not. He would work for the training.

They liked his confidence and decided to hire him on those conditions. And by the way, he immediately liked the owner/boss. They hit it off right away. Well, you guessed it. **Blessing number 10**.

Pete got the job and by the time I got home he had two weeks until he started his new job. And in the meantime, the church received an offering for us along with checks from several friends and family members that sustained us through that transition period.

That is not coincidental my friends! As I write this, I can once again say that God was truly aware of every situation that was going on in my life at that time. From the hospital bill to the job situation. He cares about every detail of your life as well. Give God a chance. He loves to prove himself and he is worthy of our praise. Whichever phrase you use - from beginning to end; to the utmost; on all counts; in full measure; to the limit; to the nth degree; hook, line and sinker; in one lump sum; from head to foot; through thick and thin; unconditionally; comprehensively; he never starts a work in you, or for you, that he doesn't finish. And all who know this say AMEN!

Now my thoughts turned to getting back to church. After all this, I needed to feel the hugs of the people in my church and although they had been continually praying since the initial accident, I needed to *hear* their prayers and be uplifted. I missed the singing and hearing my pastor's messages. I wanted to feel the fellowship that I had sorely missed. We were very involved in church and I was already trying to figure out how I could help from my wheelchair. And when the doors opened and I rolled into the church, precious Pastor Gosnell said, "Here comes our special Top Gun!" (This taken from the movie, as my fixator looked like a metal weapon!) Although I must have been a pitiful looking sight with the metal rods on one side and half leg on a pillowed leg rest on the other, I immediately felt the love and knew it was where I was supposed to be.

After my complete recovery, he asked me to tell my story to the entire church. I did so without hesitation. I was able to thank them all face to face for their prayers and help, relay all the miracles that happened and once again reiterate my gratefulness to God for saving my life. I was kept alive to tell and share about God's grace and mercy and I will forever, with gladness, continue that mission.

12

I was so happy to have been able to go to church and my life now became one of readjusting. School started for Courtney and she was quite the little trooper. She was still in her cast and hobbling on her crutches and as she was attending a Christian school at the time, **blessing number 11** occurred when I found out they had arranged to pick her up and drop her off right at the house so we wouldn't be burdened.

My parents were back to help and decided to sell their house and move to Jacksonville. They said they couldn't stay in south Florida after what happened without being able to help if needed. But my joy was short lived when I returned to the hospital for a post op visit and my skin graft was infected. I was home a total of 7 days and was admitted once again. It would be almost another month before I would be home again.

I think I was even more upset than before because the first time I didn't have a choice. I was just taken to the hospital and woke up there. Now I had tasted my freedom and life seemed somewhat normal. Now this.

They performed a procedure in my room that renewed the graft and pumped me full of antibiotics. Now it was a waiting game. Of course, prayers began again. People who know me already know why I am such a believer in divine intervention. And now you know why. I have a reason to be thankful. After another month, the infection cleared up, the graft was healing normally and I was able to return home.

The next hurdle was waiting on the swelling to go down so that I could be fit for a prosthesis. I had to wear tight socks on 'Stumpy' to help quicken the process. Residual limb sounded so medical and the layman term is stump which I didn't like, so the kids came up with Stumpy! Much lighter and fun for us when talking with them. Until then, I was in my wheelchair for the next two months. I figured out some unconventional ways to do things so I felt I was contributing and when it was time to receive my new leg, I was more than ready.

13

My parents were back home in south Florida trying to sell their house, my aunt left and Pete continued to be an exemplary employee so that he could preserve his new position.

Had it not been for **blessing number 12**, I would have been stuck indoors in my wheelchair. The men from our church were preparing to build a ramp for me over our steps to the front door. As they were discussing materials, etc., we received a call from the Workers Compensation lady that they would pay for all materials and would hire and pay for a contractor to build one for me. Now I was able to go outside for fresh air and God time without asking for help at every turn. And it was a much needed and helpful tool for the transportation drivers to and from appointments. I was to start therapy and prosthetic fittings soon and had the next question to deal with. Who would watch Brittany during the day when I was gone to appointments? The church ladies did a wonderful job of taking Brittany and both girls in a pinch, but I needed a permanent plan. I called the hospital social worker for help.

Nannies PRN was the name I was given of an agency that employed sitters for children and now we had the undaunted task of choosing someone to watch Brittany when I started leaving for appointments. She would also be watching Courtney after school if the appointments were in the afternoon. It wasn't quite as scary as it is now, but no matter the recommendations or background checks, no one wants to leave their children with a stranger. The manager asked what my preferences were. I told her I preferred a Christian woman, a mother herself, someone who was patient with children and a non-smoker due to my allergy issues. Of course, I prayed and asked God to bring the right person because I was VERY picky and these needs were important to me.

The manager ran through a list of people and selected three women that had worked for the agency awhile. I interviewed the first candidate with Brittany there to see if there was a connection. Brittany was understandably clingier to me since the accident, and I was hoping the task of choosing someone wouldn't be too difficult. Although the woman seemed nice, the interaction wasn't to my liking.

The woman from the agency sent a second prospect. Her name was Hattie and she was very soft spoken and polite, and Brittany and I immediately fell in love with her. She said she loved the Lord and was not ashamed to say so. I can tell you I was about to hire her right then and there! She said she had been a nanny before and never indulged in smoking or drinking. She also had children, and said she treated any of the children in her care as if they were her own. Brittany actually felt so comfortable with her, she climbed up in her lap as she was speaking. I couldn't believe it.

We must have talked off the work subject for over an hour. We were like two peas in a pod. After she left, I called the manager of the agency and told her I wanted 'Ms. Hattie' as the girls came to call her and there was no need for a third interview. It was a done deal. **Blessing number 13**.

God foresaw my perfect match. Earlier I said Brittany was fine physically in the accident, but her trauma was recognized later. When we would go outside for a ride in my wheelchair, Brittany would cry and grab to get up in my lap. At first I thought she was tired and didn't want to walk. Then as Pete and I started to go on little outings, we noticed that we couldn't put her down to walk up to the door. She would scream and want to be picked up and carried away from the car. She was relating the road and cars to the accident. This took some time but eventually she no longer held so closely to us and walked alongside my wheelchair holding my hand; all the while, Hattie was comforting all of us.

Later, I was made aware of another reason Hattie was so compassionate. One day she approached me about something that was bothering her. She asked if her daughter could be dropped off at my house after school. She drove to the north side of town and because of heavy traffic was getting to her school late after leaving me. She didn't want to be an imposition and said, if not, she would work it out. We were friends by then, not employer and nanny, and I thought it was a great idea. She could play with Courtney as well when she got home from school.

Then she added, "I want you to know my daughter is mentally challenged and I will understand if you say no". I could see the love she had for her daughter and that made me love her that much more. From the start, both of my girls loved Hattie and now they enjoyed waiting for her daughter's bus to arrive. She was a welcome addition to their afternoons while waiting for me to return. Hattie played with them, took care of my house and sat after hours to read bible verses with me when I was down or hurting.

There was no doubt in my mind that God knew exactly what he was doing when he paired us together.

14

After a few more months, we were summoned by the Sherriff's office to come and talk to the police officer who first responded to my accident. A neighbor near the accident scene had seen the hit and run driver slipping over the fence in her backyard. She alerted the police who later found the young man hiding in the attic of the home he was moving from.

When questioned by the officer, he showed no remorse for the pain he had caused to me and my girls. He was only worried that I was deceased and that a manslaughter conviction would mean he would be in jail longer. Since this was his third DWI offense, (don't know if anyone was hurt prior to me) he knew the sentencing process and lengths of prison time. And because there was no way to test for marijuana after they found him, they couldn't use the lit remains as evidence for more charges. The police officer was clearly frustrated by all this and apologized for what we had been through.

As he was talking, I noticed that he had my driver's license blown up and pinned to the backboard over his desk. Ladies, as we all know, a driver's license picture isn't usually the best, but blown up, oh my! I asked him why he kept the copy of it. He explained that when they were taking me to the hospital the ambulance driver said I probably wouldn't make it due to the severity of my injuries. When people die, he felt like he could relate to them better in court by studying their picture and reminding himself that this was a mother, wife, or daughter of someone and they were special. I was so taken aback by the kindness in his eyes while telling me this, that I began to cry and forgot all about the 8 X 10 photocopy to which he was referring. Then he said he didn't need it now because I was here. That was a great feeling. I was still in a wheelchair, but I was alive!

He said we would be called into court before a judge with the young man for sentencing and it would help for the judge to hear what I wanted to say. I said I would and now we waited for the hearing date.

The day came and Pete and I were taken into a courtroom with only a handful of people in the room. A clerk showed us where to sit. As the judge entered, I looked to my right and saw a young man with his head down, not showing any emotion, and a man beside him at a table.

The officer of the court read my name vs. ____. Yes, I still remember his name, but will refer to him as the young man, and the judge began. He read the charges for him – "Leaving the scene of an accident involving death or injury".

(I found out later that had he stayed at the scene, he would have only been charged with reckless driving and been sent home with a ticket.)

Then the judge turned to me, said he was very sorry this had happened to me and asked if there was anything I would like to say to him or the young man. I said I did. I turned to the young man who remained looking downward. I told him it was very hard for me to go on and the life that I once knew was now impossible. If I could turn back the hands of time that day and not been there with my girls, I would gladly do so. I also added that he needed to realize that his lack of good judgement that day had affected many others other than himself. He would do his time and then return to his regular lifestyle, while I could not. I hoped he could comprehend the magnitude and significance that his decisions caused and that there would always be consequences for his actions. Then I told him I forgave him because I knew that he didn't plan to hit us and injure us as he did. Then I finished.

I hadn't noticed because I was looking at the young man, but the judge had taken his glasses off and was wiping his eyes. He cleared his throat, put his glasses back on and proceeded to look towards the young man. His voice sounded so kind to me, but now he was all business. He told the young man to look at him as he was being sentenced. He looked up and the judge spoke. "If it was up to me", he said, "I would sentence you with much more, but I can only give you what the law allows". He would serve 103 days in the county jail, then serve probation for 5 years. Within 30 days of release he was to get a full-time job or show proof of employer contacts to his parole officer. Also, he was to pay $200 a month in restitution to us for our injuries. Other provisions which applied were gone over such as no intoxicants, rules for his supervision, etc.

Most of these I knew were merely words written down. I didn't believe he would listen or adhere to them, but hoped and prayed he wouldn't be irresponsible forever or hurt someone else. But I felt better forgiving him because it is clear that when you are a Christian you are to forgive others (Colossians 3:13 - "Make allowances for each other's faults, and forgive anyone who offends you. Remember, the Lord forgave you, so you must forgive others".) And even if you are not a believer, when you don't forgive it only bothers you and eats away at any pure happiness you could have. The other person who has offended you probably doesn't care how you feel about them. They are moving on. But your hurt can turn to anger quickly and be aimed toward someone else when not even meaning to.

Not only did it make me feel released from the hurt, but I knew he heard me; and perhaps at some point in his life he would accept Jesus and remember my words.

As it turned out, he was released after two months, skipped his parole meeting, left town and was recaptured and sent to a state prison without paying the remaining restitution. As a victim, I was sent notification 3 years later that he was up for parole and would I like to say anything about his possibility for parole. I responded saying that maybe part of his parole conditions should be volunteering in the trauma unit of the hospital so that he could realize the devastation caused to families by wrong choices behind the wheel of a car. (Now that we have cell phones, texting while driving has now been added to the list of choices causing chaos and death).

I still pray that someone came into his life that made an impact on him and showed him how much better things can be if he has Jesus in his life. It can't be explained, it can only be experienced. The good thing about Jesus is he doesn't wait for you to change. He takes you as you are and loves you without condition. Maybe, just maybe, he is using *his* story to help others who have an addiction to make a change. Never underestimate the power of your story, good or bad. God can use it for a mighty purpose.

15

After the sentencing, I tried to put as much of the accident behind me as I could, but many "ifs" crept through my mind for several years. If I would have taken a break when my daughter asked to go get a drink; if I had only chosen to take the delivery job one day instead of two; if I had done the job on my own without taking the girls along, on and on and on. I struggled with doing things differently and slower. I struggled with looking different and not having the nice shaped legs I had before (yes, a little vanity there, but those were normal thoughts from a wounded woman's standpoint). It is always a good thing to have a good self-image of yourself, but from the inside out not the other way around. Then I finally realized that I kept telling God that I was so grateful for being alive, but was I really?

There are many stages to any loss that occurs. Sadness, anger, self-pity, depression, and/or denial, but then hopefully perseverance and acceptance. I would just have moments when I would cry and cry for no reason, wishing I could change that day and have the life I had before. Those feelings are all very normal and part of the process of moving on. Of course, I still wish it hadn't happened, but the one thing I never did was to blame God for what happened. I know as a Christian that God *allows* things to happen for His plans and purposes, but never *causes* the bad things. All I knew was I was not going to let this beat me. I had two beautiful children and a husband who were counting on me.

I had one follow up with the surgeon, which was wonderful. I told him I could never praise him enough and that God sent him to me that day. He, of course, said that's why he became a surgeon and was very humble about the whole thing. I relayed to him that my life could have taken a much different turn had it not been for him, **BUT** God had other plans.

I was then sent to the plastic surgeon to make sure everything was finalized with him. If you remember, he was the one that sent the psychologist in and who also suggested that I may perhaps have to have a bone graft if it didn't heal right. At this visit I reminded him what he said while I was in the hospital and that I knew I wouldn't need it. He had to agree as he could visually see the x-rays where the bone was indeed solid and strong. I don't know if he believed that the Lord had a hand in the healing, but he certainly saw the difference in what he had believed and what actually occurred. I was happy for the somewhat skeptical look, as I hoped that would bring questions into his mind about how I never had been in denial. I had only been confident in my Savior's ability.

As I began my slow journey to recovery, someone suggested that I buy a journal and document every little step towards my progress. That was the best suggestion I ever had. The first few months were hard, mentally and physically. The very first day I was upright, I was only able to take steps from my room to the end of our hallway, about 9 feet. I was exhausted and frustrated. The Lord had a lot of work to do in me as far as patience was concerned.

As I wrote in my journal and time went on, I did see a progression, albeit a slight one. Day two was walking to the front door. Day three - walking down the ramp. Day four - to the end of the driveway. Although to anyone else these steps were minute, they were giant achievements for me. Hattie helped me take walks that eventually got me to the end of our street and back. Monumental!

In my independent mind, I thought I should have been walking around the block, but through the journaling I saw that those little steps led up to the big ones. When people say baby steps…. that's a real and good thing. It built muscle, endurance and patience. The other progressions were from wheelchair to walker, then to crutches, then cane and then no assistance. This took time and I had plenty of that. Eventually, I was able to resume my full-time job as mommy and let Hattie move on to help another person in need. This was so hard for me to do, but I knew the impact she had on our lives would never be forgotten.

Ms. Hattie was with us as part of my family for almost a year, until I was able to walk without assistance and drive again. In 2013, I reunited with her again and took Brittany along. She was still just as wonderful and we had lunch and enjoyed catching up on a lot of lost years. I showed her a picture of her and Brittany as a baby and took a picture of them now. And to confirm her love of her 'children', she also had a picture in her wallet that she brought of Brittany and Courtney. Folks like that are just hard to find, and I know God will reward her greatly for all that she meant to our family.

16

It was now June 22, 1991, and the anniversary of my accident. I decided to bake some goodies and visit the fire station where the men were that rescued me. Because the shifts change from day to day, I wasn't sure "C" shift would be there. If they were there, would any of the men who came to my rescue remember me?

I found the fire station and knocked on the door. When the door opened, there stood a very tall firefighter that filled the doorway. I explained about my accident the previous year and I thought the men who came that day needed to be reminded how much they meant to me. I said it was "C" shift and was anyone there that may have been there and remembered. He didn't speak for a moment, and then he said. "**I** was there. You're the lady that was hit by the car with your little girls, right? And you lost your leg!" Then he looked down toward my leg and seemed surprised that I was walking. I smiled and answered "yes, that's me". Then he continued. "I remember you. When we saw the condition of your legs, we couldn't believe that there was hardly any blood loss". I questioned him about that statement because I knew nothing about what had anatomically gone on. He said, "You see, ma'am, both of your main arteries were severed. Usually when an accident like that happens, by the time we get there the victim is deceased because of the blood loss. But in your case, when we looked at your legs, it looked like your arteries had sealed themselves shut. Almost like a time-lapse photo of a plant stem that curls under to close. I've never seen anything like it in my 20+ years in this profession. And you were praying really loud about saving your life!"

Well, then I had a chance to answer with what I knew. I said, "Well, you know that wasn't a coincidence, right? God had other plans for me and you all were his hands on the ground". He smiled and said, "It was something miraculous for sure".

I wasn't able to meet all of the "C" shift firefighters that helped me the day of my accident, but met other wonderful men. I had a wonderful visit, gave them the baked goods and returned home. I had just heard **Blessing Number 14**. God had once again given me a glimpse of his wonderful power through the eyes of another who was there to see; and the fact that he remembered from a year ago, spoke volumes. Maybe walking in on a whim was a testimony without even knowing it. God is so good!

17

We had a routine working now that was as normal as could be. Pete's job was working out well, I was homeschooling both girls and we were once again trying for another child. I prayed this time for a little boy, since I probably wouldn't have more children after this due to the hardships with the prosthetic leg. Not having a prosthetic leg, you probably aren't aware of how the fitting process works. With a prosthetic leg, you have to make sure your weight gain or loss is minimal. If you stay within 10 pounds either way, the effect of the fit of your leg would typically not be affected. That's hard to do when you become pregnant. I was already off balance so to speak, as I couldn't depend on a sturdy foot for stability.

I specifically prayed for a boy as Hannah did in the bible. I told God that if I could have a son, I would give him over completely for God to use in a mighty way. My God is a God of details. He decides the outcomes, but he delights in honoring the prayers of his children. I also had my MOPS group praying with me and several of my closest friends at church who knew we were trying. Be specific when you pray.

You will be surprised at the preciseness of the answers God will give.

I found out in the beginning of November that I was indeed expecting. We were elated. Then in February, we found out that it was a little boy! **Blessing number 15**! Whether or not you choose to believe that outcomes are divine or not, I hope you will believe that God cares about you and already knows your desires, before you speak them. In my case, I know God heard my prayer. On July 6th, we had our third child, Zachary. It is a variation of Zachariah, which means, 'whom God remembers'. And that was certainly fitting for us as well.

Our lives were shaping back into a family and I began to assimilate into my life as an amputee. Zack was my answered prayer for sure and because he was born after my amputation, he didn't view me as different in any way. He only knew when his mommy needed her leg, he would pick it up (it was a heavy item for my little toddler) and bring it to me to put on. My disability was a very ordinary thing to him. Courtney, my oldest, became a mini me and jumped to the challenge, helping tremendously with her younger siblings and Brittany helped by playing mama on a real live doll! I actually began to forget all the bad things and was able to focus on my little family and all of the things I *could* do; and was able to do because I was alive to do them! I actually went to our church fall festival as a pirate's mate using my fake leg. Perfect, right?

Come on, you have to have some humor to get along with things you can't change. Like the time Pete suggested, while we were at the beach, that I take my leg off in the water and scream "SHARK"! Okay, of course I didn't do that, but you have to have a positive attitude and a broader perspective of the circumstance. The circumstance itself can beat you if you let negative thoughts enter into your mind. This is, by the way, Satan's favorite place to occupy. If he can get you to believe thoughts like, I am damaged goods, poor me, no one will see me as normal, I can never do (blank) again so why try? etc., etc., you can and will defeat yourself before you even have a significant chance to achieve your highest potential.

It's crucial that you be surrounded with family and friends that will be honest with you and not join your pity party. I'm not saying that sometimes we just need a shoulder to lean on or a warm embrace with no words spoken. Believe me, I had plenty of moments of sorrow, regret and self-doubt. But I had family members, my husband in particular, that could snap me back out of it with heartfelt comments and words of encouragement.

With each day, something would take me back to remember what had happened, how far I had come from just a few years earlier with God's help, and how thankful I was that I was here to be a wife and mom to three beautiful children. Then another thought entered my mind, and if I had let my own thoughts of inadequacy and ignorance of how to do something come into play, the next miracle would never have been possible. Believe you can do it, and pray constantly for something that means a lot to you. God will hear. He wants to do great things for you. And if God has a hand in it and it's in his plans, it will happen, and bigger and better than you can imagine. Then give Him the acknowledgement and honor that is due Him for all the wonderful things that come to pass. Take it from someone who has seen his miracles. It really does work!

18

The question that was troubling me was this. There must be other people like me and if so, how are they dealing with losing a limb? Was there a group or association that helped amputees and their families? If there was, I wasn't told of one. I knew of groups for diabetes, cystic fibrosis, muscular dystrophy, multiple sclerosis, the heart association, and on and on. But nothing in my big city for limb loss. And as I found out later, because it is a big city, there were more amputees than I could have imagined. Many were shut ins and elderly. The doctors helped while you were in the hospital to get you well enough to leave. Then there was no outside help to aid you in your home environment.

I learned that you could shower standing up without a stool, but you had to have a certain cover so the prosthesis wouldn't get water in its working parts. And you had to be careful to wear shoes, even at the beach. Any sharp object could poke or tear the 'skin' covering your leg, thus letting in water or sand and damaging or clogging the internal parts.

There were special accessories to help you get the right fit so your residual limb wouldn't get blisters, and you do get blisters. To a lay person, the closest explanation I could use as to how a prosthesis feels, would be to walk on your knees holding your legs up behind you as you did as a child to be funny. It was only fun for a while, then it started to hurt. That's what the life of a lower limb amputee is.

There were differences in the types of legs you could have. Some had movable ankles so women could wear high heels and flats. They could be shaped to match your other leg and then sprayed with a coating that looked and felt like real skin, minus the hair which women don't want anyway! And artificial nails could be added and painted to match your real foot. It was so wonderful and much more advanced than I had envisioned.

I learned that area rugs were dangerous for a leg amputee. One wrinkle that you are no longer able to feel, could be devastating, possibly fatal. You should always be aware of the material you are walking on. You can't feel a crack in a sidewalk, loose pebbles on a road, or, heaven help you, a wet spot on the ceramic tile in the mall! These were all new to me, but I learned them by trial and error. It would have been much better if someone had told me.

Then I had an idea. I asked Pete what he thought about starting a support group for amputees. Even though I didn't know how I would start, where I would hold the meetings or how to contact anybody, he was in. I decided on the name

A.B.L.E. It stood for Amputees Believing Life is Exciting. So, with much prayer our new adventure began.

I started by contacting the Disabled Services division in our city. I talked to the secretary to Jack Gillrup, Chief of Disabled Services, and told her my intentions. She was delighted to hear someone wanted to have a group to help. She said she would relay the message and ask him to call me. Within a couple of days, he contacted me and I gave him all the suggestions I had and what I wanted to do. My objective was to speak to amputees and their families so they might all gain knowledge. Also, I wanted to have events for the whole family that would be fun but perhaps still push the patient beyond their comfort zone. I explained that I didn't have a facility to have the meetings, but once I did I would go into the hospitals to talk with doctors, nurses and physical therapists, meet new amputees and leave a card and flyers with information if the patients had further questions.

If an amputee had come to talk to me while I was in the hospital, I have no doubt it would have made a greater impact on my recuperation and emotional state. Referring back to an earlier statement - if you have experienced something first hand, there is no one better to explain and encourage another while coping with the same hurt.

<u>Blessing number 16</u>. Immediately after I explained my vision, he said he thought he could help me; but I never imagined how much. He said to come meet him the next day to look at a meeting facility. He used it for community events and charity conferences and thought it may work for me. I couldn't believe it. This man knew nothing about me but was already willing to give me a place to hold meetings with new amputees. Could it be God at work? Of course. And after meeting this wonderful man who was a quadriplegic himself, I was given the keys to the facility and told I could use it any Saturday I wanted.

I may not have mentioned this other attribute of God, but he tends to be an on-time God. It was as if God had timed the thought process of helping amputees with the availability and location ahead of time just for me. And the location was 3.3 miles from my home! I wouldn't have to rush to drive an extensive distance with my family. I wanted the patient's family to come, not just the amputees themselves. Families are affected as well and this would be a great place to meet and plan. I was over the moon with excitement!

I started making a pamphlet with the ABLE name and making business cards to pass out. I was able to get my prosthetist, Mike Richard on board to help make his other patients aware and to talk to the doctors he worked with. I went back to the hospital to see the sweet D.O.N who had been with me been for so long and she gave the cards to the nurses.

Before the initial group meeting I was determined to push myself a little if I expected others who may come to do the same. I decided to enter a 5-mile walkathon for diabetes, which was the diagnosis for my mother. I was only able to walk about 1 mile, but this one incident was the first significant achievement to give me confidence and proved to myself that with the Lord's help, I would be able to do what I put my mind to. Then a local television anchor interviewed me about the walkathon and my recovery, and when the story aired and a newspaper article was published, it helped get the word out as well.

Now all I had to do was plan my list of events and dates and wait. More practicing the patience thing. I admit I am still learning that one. But I was also praying that God would send the people that needed this the most and that I would be able to help them in some way. What I didn't want was for the meetings/events to be "woe is me", and "I'll never be able to do that again". It goes back to not telling me I *can't* do something. I wanted them to feel empowered by their own triumphs, however big or small they may be. This is the attitude I wanted to convey from the start and still be sensitive to people's desires and capabilities. Now it was in God's hands.

19

The first kick off of the ABLE group was here. I planned a light menu for the meet and greet, with danish, fruit, muffins and drinks. I received calls from three different families, so although I was nervous, at least I knew someone would be there. I was hoping that the families would see that even though they had a disability they could overcome it, and being with others could open up a whole new world for them.

As they began to arrive, I realized that this social gathering was very diversified. That was great! There was a senior amputee who came with his bride of 50+ years and they reminded me of my grandparents whom I adored, an enthusiastic young man of 9 with his mother, a middle-aged man who was an above elbow amputee, and another man about 22 who was a bilateral AK amputee, (double amputee above the knee). These four attendees and their families became regulars and part of my extended family. All ages, all ethnicities, very unique personalities and all with different stories to tell. They all wanted to share their experiences and all seemed excited to begin our adventures together.

After I introduced myself and my family, they each introduced themselves and communicated what they had in mind for the group. They shared what they wished to learn from it and how they thought they could help. I couldn't have asked for a better first meeting. I loved them all from the start and I immediately told them of the outings and speakers planned for our group. I planned cookouts at local parks, para-sailing, hiking, horseback riding, a trip to our local dinner theater and different guest speakers (doctors, prosthetists, etc.) who could answer other questions that I could not. I was overwhelmed that it was off to such a great start.

For those of you reading that don't know me, I am certainly not an introvert. I am very outgoing and I love to meet new people. I also like to help others when I can. That is what makes me tick, so to speak. But everyone is different, and that's ok. That's how God made us. The young college student was the shyest and quietest one in our group. He was very personable but needed a little space to listen and feel accepted. He was pursuing his degree in Criminal Justice and had no family in town. He had one big smile, however, that couldn't be missed. He did remarkably well and made it clear he did what he could on his own without assistance.

That is a hard thing for families to learn when their loved one loses a limb. They feel so heartbroken that they want to help with everything. Those intentions are wonderful and to have a family or friends to support you is one of the best things you can have. However, if you aren't given the opportunity to try to do things, you may never be able to achieve your potential simply because there is no reason to make the effort. I believe that applies to life in general, not just to disabilities. Don't become lazy and for goodness sake, don't give up or depend on others until you have tried your very best to accomplish the task. Then if you can't possibly reach the goal, don't be afraid to ask for help. Hopefully someone will be there and welcome the chance to assist you.

Mike wanted to be independent to a point. His purpose for coming to the meetings was for social interaction with people who could understand his issues as an amputee and help him to go beyond what he thought he could accomplish. That was exactly what I hoped for. Sometimes he needed a little boost of encouragement but he always ended up putting his best effort into whatever was being presented. He was certainly an inspiration to me.

To add a little side note, this was evidenced in two of our events that I will never forget. He rode a horse for the first time, and it required help for him to ride on the horse without limbs to balance. He was very nervous but afterward said he couldn't wait to show his mom the picture we took. I loved the cheesy grin! And when para sailing, once again, special arrangements were put in place to assist him in the harness while leaving the boat deck. A little apprehensive, but daring to push beyond his fear, he sailed high over the river. Everyone was cheering him on as we heard him whooping and hollering his excitement. This was what these events were all about. Accomplishing something and proving to yourself… YOU ARE CAPABLE!

Robert and his wife were very active in the group and very helpful. He had lost his arm in an accident and had been an amputee for a while. His wife was quiet and caring and was used to his constant joking. His personality just drew people to him and he always lifted the spirits of others around him. He was invaluable to me as occasionally he would visit new male patients for me as the occasions arose. He was perfect for the job and he was usually one of the first to sign up for the A.B.L.E. activities.

Max and his wife were as sweet as could be. They enjoyed the company of the people in the group and always made themselves available if I needed something. They were, as I said, my 'adopted' grandparents and took on that role to all of us, especially to our youngest member, Bobby. Their devotion to each other and to the group was evident to all who met them.

Bobby was a bundle of energy and wanted to do anything and everything I could think of. He had absolutely no fear and never let his disability prevent him from a challenge.

He already ran in local running events and his mother was a stalwart supporter and his biggest fan at every event.

I was more than ecstatic that a mere thought was actually coming to fruition in such a spectacular fashion. But I knew that God was in charge and that he was the reason it was such a huge success.

We had many excursions and had many more families join after that. From all kind of incidents, (alligator attacks to motorcycle accidents) and from all walks of life, (policemen and grandmothers) we grew as a family.

After a year as Founder of A.B.L.E, I was awarded the Celebrate Independence Award given to those people and organizations that have made a difference in the lives of the disabled. They awarded five individuals and five companies. They were absolutely awe inspiring people with varying stories and different reasons why they wanted to help and never seeking any gratification for themselves. I was truly humbled. It was a shining moment for mankind and proved these things still occur and I'm sure all of the nominees felt as I did at the end of the night. While I was honored and thrilled that someone had thought enough of my efforts to put my name in as a possible nominee, I didn't expect or need a plaque or special recognition. After all, my purpose from the very start was to be of help to someone.

I made many new friends in the five years I held my support group but as life became more hectic with all the activities that go along with three children, I was no longer able to continue the group. It was, however, a life changing experience with many treasured memories and one for which I will be forever thankful to have been a part.

20

I don't know if perk is the word to use, but one of the definitions of perk is a benefit or special advantage; and some opportunities began to arise for me that I would call perks. From meeting those wonderful people there, I was invited to a ski clinic in Killington, Vermont a year later. It was completely free to all first-time amputees. All expenses paid for Pete and myself for four days. Perk? I think so. They fit you with adaptive ski equipment, administered lessons and then on the last day, actually planned a downhill ski race just like the Olympics, starting gate and all. I met many more families and began to realize there are indeed other people willing to help with this disability, so the amputee can live life to their fullest potential.

From there I was informed that there would be try outs in Jacksonville for the Paralympics. Not skiing of course for this Florida girl, but I signed up not knowing what to expect but willing to give it my best and push my limits. As it turned out, I tried out for track and field for the javelin, discus and shot put. I couldn't quite get the running then but made county finals, then state, and went on to compete in the Nationals in Maryland. I did win second place in my division, although I didn't score high enough to make the Paralympics. But just to compete was an honor and a wonderful memory.

I have just passed my 26th year as an amputee and I guess I can say I am a veteran amputee now. I have conquered hiking mountains, swimming, biking, bowling, and many other challenges and am still ready and willing to help with information about the ups and downs of being what I call *'handi-capable'*, not handicapped. Its relearning or what I define as this: the redirection of performing skills you once managed, in a new and somewhat challenging way.

As recently as a month ago, I received a call from the mother of a young lady named Jennifer, who remembered me visiting her daughter in the hospital when she was a teen going through losing a limb. She contacted me for any information I could convey that may help amputees like us. Like me, they are compassionate about the quality of life people can enjoy. They simply want to provide opportunities for amputees to interact with their peers while performing activities in a fun and compassionate setting. Jennifer has started a nonprofit with the assistance of her mother Charlene, called Amputee Fitness Council, Inc. Jennifer chose the trademark name 'Ampunique', which I believe is an aptly fitting name for a wonderfully unique group of people. I foresee good things coming for our community through their efforts, and know this much-needed organization will be a God send for those searching for help.

As is our life as a human, we will have a lifetime of challenges, good or bad. They can be a time of learning, healing and growing; and hopefully as you meet them head on, you will be able to use your previous experiences to help you move forward when the next glitch in life comes your way.

One of those so-called glitches happened to me in 2008. I tripped and landed full force on my prosthetic leg, breaking my knee on my amputated limb. Although this was a setback, I thought back to what I had been through previously and realized this too would pass. Now I am dealing with other health issues, but God was faithful before my accident and continues to be faithful to me still. My blessings continue every day.

21

Although that part of my life is a memory now, there have been other situations that have been a challenge for me, but God has never let me down, and He will never let you down.

In the beginning of my book, I mentioned that if you did not know the Lord, I would let you in on a simple prayer that will not only help you with life in general, but will also put you in God's hands and make you a child of his forever. God's son Jesus died for you because he loves you and he has always been with you, waiting for this day. Perhaps you feel alone, misunderstood, or are in a situation that you can't control. That doesn't mean He isn't there. He can and will always be there for you to lean on. He takes you as you are. He is only concerned with the condition of your heart. He wants you to realize that you need him, because he already knows what you need before you even ask. He doesn't *need* us.

When we are heartbroken and come to Him with a sincere heart, he is always ready and delighted to help. It is all about believing in your heart that Jesus is Lord. It's as simple as ABC. You only have to 1) **<u>Admit you are a sinner</u>**, (you are not alone in that one). Romans 3:23 says we have <u>ALL</u> sinned and come short of the glory of God. No one is perfect except Jesus. 2) **<u>Believe that Jesus is God's son</u>** and because he loved us so much he sent his son to die for our sins. (Romans 5:8). He was born to a virgin, died and was buried, three days later rose from the grave and went to heaven and is waiting to take us there one day. And 3) **<u>Confess your sins and ask Jesus into your heart and be Lord of your life</u>**. That's it. Isn't that simple? There is no other way to be 'saved'. God was the one who created us, so it makes sense that only God can save us, and he chose Jesus as the way to do that.

When we repent, Luke 15:10 tell us that there is joy in the presence of God's angels when only one repents. Repenting is having a sincere heart. To be *truly* sorry and want to start again, trying hard not to commit the same sins. (You can only try your best. Remember you aren't perfect, you are human.) God understands when we fail and fall again. He is loving and will forgive over and over again. You don't need to know any fancy prayers, just talk to Him as you would your best friend because He is your very best friend.

When you do this, the bible says you are a new creature; the old has passed away and the new has come. This means that anyone who belongs to Christ has become a new person. Your old life is gone and a new one has begun! And then God's gift to us is living with Him eternally in heaven (Romans 6:23).

Then you may say you will say the prayer later and think about it. Why should you ask Him into your heart now? The devil knows that if you wait, the next day may not come. We don't have control of what each day holds. And then it's too late.

You can simply say, "Lord, please forgive me, for I'm a sinner. I believe you are the son of God, and died on the cross for my sins. I want you to come into my heart and be Lord of my life forever. (Romans 10:13 assures us of this… "For <u>everyone</u> who calls on the name of the Lord <u>will</u> be saved".

I know it seems like a simple prayer to change a mountain of difficulties, but that's just how our God is. He doesn't use complex methods. He uses the simple, everyday things so as mere humans we can understand. He sent Jesus as a little baby and that baby has forever changed our world.

I pray that you see the urgent need to accept Jesus and you prayed those words. If you are still unsure, find a bible based church and tell the pastor. He will be excited to pray with you and tell you other wonderful things about becoming a Christian!

We were not made to walk alone. Don't be embarrassed or ashamed to ask for help. This is the first step to a new and changed life for you. All of us were in your place at one time and have made that confession of faith. We humbled ourselves, got real with the Lord, and chose to follow Him; and there is no better feeling than to feel free and unburdened from guilt and shame. Jesus is the pro when it comes to lifting burdens.

After that, you will want to tell everyone about your new experience! That one decision will be the most important thing that ever happens in your life. You may see a miraculous change overnight, but more than likely things may seem to get harder for a bit than easier. Make no mistake that Satan, or the devil, is real. It is not a hocus pocus thing. He wants the total opposite of what Jesus wants for you. He is called the Father of Lies, and he's very good at it.

I mentioned the bible verse that says his sole purpose is to steal, kill and destroy. If he can get you to believe that nothing will ever change and that your life is the way it will always be, he will continue to destroy your life. That's because Satan doesn't want you to believe anything great has really happened to you. Don't believe the lies. I could have wallowed in self-pity and never wanted to go out into the world or see people again (and I met people who felt exactly that way). But because of Jesus, I had a completely different perspective. I KNEW I would conquer it. I KNEW he would help me. It's called Faith.

There is an unseen world that surrounds us. But that doesn't mean it's not there. An example was used one time of the wind. You can't see it with your eye, but you know it's there by what it does. The same is true about Jesus. You may not physically see Him, but you will notice things being different; things improving or good things going on that you can't explain. That's God. He will always be there for you. And because he is not human, he doesn't have conditions. He doesn't wait until you become a better person, clean up, become free of addictions, or not love you because of your past. When you ask Him to be Lord of your life, he forgets your past. As I said before, he's been there all along, waiting patiently. (Jeremiah 29:11 – "<u>For I know the plans I have for you</u>," declares the Lord, "<u>plans to prosper you and not harm you, plans to give you hope and a future</u>."

When you make the decision to accept Jesus, please let me know. I will rejoice with you! HOW EXCITING! My pastor says that as a Christian, we are no better than anyone else, just better off; and I believe that's true.

Now, my hope is this: that you found comfort and encouragement from this book and have renewed expectations for a brighter future. I pray you will make that commitment and not only receive the confident assurance of an everlasting life with a loving Savior, but many blessings to come as you begin your new life in Christ! And remember, you are special and never alone!

Acknowledgements

(In order of sequence)

My hubby, Pete - Once again I want to acknowledge my wonderful husband. He has been through many things with me throughout our 32 years of marriage and continues to be my rock. Thank you, Pete, for your encouragement, love and support; and speaking what I *need* to hear even when it may not be what I *want* to hear. I love you with all my heart. You are amazing!

To my awesome children, Courtney, Brittany and Zachary – I am so thankful that the Lord chose to save my life and honor me with the privilege of being your mama. I love you with all my heart and pray God will continue to pour out his blessings on each of you!

Jeff Lott – Jeff and the crew of the Jacksonville Fire and Rescue Station #20 were sent to help me that day, and I can't praise them enough. He also came to the hospital to check on me with his fellow firefighters and left a sweet card that

I still have. They will be etched in my mind forever for the compassion they displayed.

Pastor Weldon and **Betty Gosnell,** and **Pastor Rick** and **Sherree Crook** – these were my two incredible pastors and their wives, who led a family of believers that truly were my second family. So many people reached out to us, I can't thank the entire church body by name, but you know who you are.

Terri Hudson, Sharon Grady and Linda Alvarez – these Girl Scout moms were instrumental in encouraging me and showing me they still counted on and needed me as a leader. They helped the girls to see no differences in a person with a disability.

Gae Cavanagh – Gae was our MOPS mama and spiritual leader, and still is a mighty prayer warrior for everyone. I want to thank her and all the moms who prayed for me during my difficult recovery. Those uplifting prayers got me through many long days and were very appreciated.

Hattie Demps – Hattie was not only a caregiver for my children, she was also my friend. Because of her unwavering faith and devotion to the Lord, my faith and strength were renewed daily, which I believe helped accelerate my recuperation. She is with the Lord now but I will never forget her; and I am so glad God let us meet this side of heaven.

Jack Gillrup, Former Chief of Disabled Services - His compassion and willingness to accommodate people with disabilities was evident to me from my first meeting with him. I will always remember his kindness to me and helping to make my idea come alive.

Mike Richard, CPO & Owner of Advance Prosthetics and Orthotics - Mike was a huge supporter of the idea of the A.B.L.E. group from its conception, and helped me tremendously with event participation and publicity. He has been my prosthetist for 20+ years and is passionate about helping amputees achieve their goals and live fuller lives beyond amputation.

Jennifer Simms and Charlene Hixon – Founders of Amputee Fitness Council, Inc. They are committed to bringing quality opportunities to individuals who have lost a limb. Their focus is to serve. I am so impressed with their drive and consideration for others and hope to help get the word out so their group grows by leaps and bounds.

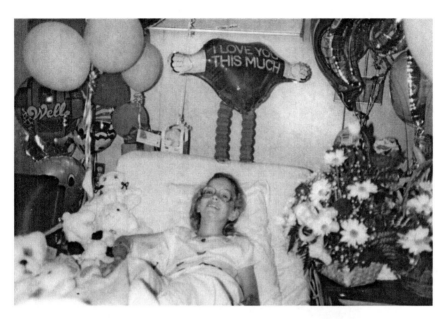

Courtney recovering in the hospital.

Attending a friend's wedding and Courtney was the junior bridesmaid.

Ms. Hattie and Brittany.

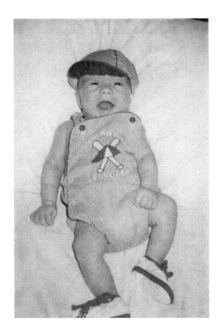

Baby Zachary.

My first family outing walking with my prosthesis.

Pete and I attending the ski clinic in Vermont.

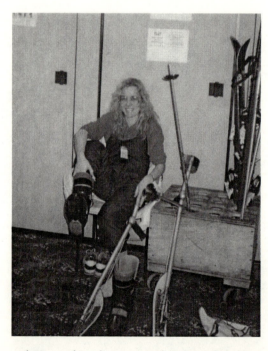

Preparing to brave the slopes with my adaptive equipment

Zachary bringing me the discus in preparation for the Paralympic trials in Maryland.

Receiving my medals at the completion of the Track and Field competition.

At an outing with the ABLE group.

An excited Mike riding a horse for the first time.

Me getting ready for the ride.

1992 family photo.

2015 family photo.
From left to right - Pete, Denise, Brittany and son, Zachary and fiancee, Taylor, and Courtney and husband, Seth and children